The Snail Tale

Mary Elizabeth Salzmann

Consulting Editor, Diane Craig, M.A./Reading Specialist

Published by ABDO Publishing Company, 4940 Viking Drive, Edina, Minnesota 55435.

Printed in the United States.

Credits
Edited by: Pam Price
Curriculum Coordinator: Nancy Tuminelly
Cover and Interior Design and Production: Mighty Media
Photo and Illustration Credits: BananaStock Ltd., Comstock, Corbis Images, Eyewire Images, Hemera, Tracy Kompelien, PhotoDisc, Stockbyte, Thinkstock

Library of Congress Cataloging-in-Publication Data

Salzmann, Mary Elizabeth, 1968-
    The snail tale / Mary Elizabeth Salzmann.
      p. cm. -- (Rhyme time)
    ISBN 1-59197-816-5 (hardcover)
    ISBN 1-59197-922-6 (paperback)
    1. English language--Rhyme--Juvenile literature. I. Title. II. Rhyme time (ABDO Publishing Company)

PE1517.S358 2004
428.1'3--dc22
                                                                              2004049106

SandCastle™ books are created by a professional team of educators, reading specialists, and content developers around five essential components that include phonemic awareness, phonics, vocabulary, text comprehension, and fluency. All books are written, reviewed, and leveled for guided reading, early intervention reading, and Accelerated Reader® programs and designed for use in shared, guided, and independent reading and writing activities to support a balanced approach to literacy instruction.

Let Us Know

After reading the book, SandCastle would like you to tell us your stories about reading. What is your favorite page? Was there something hard that you needed help with? Share the ups and downs of learning to read. We want to hear from you! To get posted on the ABDO Publishing Company Web site, send us e-mail at:

sandcastle@abdopub.com

SandCastle Level: Transitional

Words that rhyme do not have to be spelled the same. These words rhyme with each other:

gale

snail

male

stale

tale

nail

pail

trail

sail

whale

Peter's father helps him hammer
a nail.

The palm trees are being blown by a strong wind called a **gale**.

Jenny has a red pail.

Mary's dog, Buster, is **male**.

Peggy and Will and their parents like to **sail**.

After lunch, Tom will close the bread bag so the bread won't get **stale**.

Ricky is petting a **snail**.

Naomi and her dad are reading a funny **tale**.

Matt and his mom rest beside
the trail.

Jane and her dad float on
a **whale**.

The Snail Tale

This is the tale
of a male snail
named Dale.

Every day Dale
followed the trail
down to the beach
to get his mail.

One morning Dale
found a pail with a sail
sitting next to his mail.

Dale got into the pail
and went for a sail.

Suddenly, a gale
blew the pail into a nail!

19

The pail sprang a leak from the nail.
Dale tried to bail,
but water kept filling the pail.

Luckily, Dale
was friends with a whale
who gave him a ride on her tail!

Rhyming Riddle

What do you call a path just for boys and men?

trail of fun!

no GIRLS allowed

Male trail

Glossary

bail. to use a small container to scoop up and remove water

pail. bucket

snail. a small animal with a spiral shell, no legs, and a soft, slimy body

stale. no longer fresh

tale. a story that can be real or made up

About SandCastle™

A professional team of educators, reading specialists, and content developers created the SandCastle™ series to support young readers as they develop reading skills and strategies and increase their general knowledge. The SandCastle™ series has four levels that correspond to early literacy development in young children. The levels are provided to help teachers and parents select the appropriate books for young readers.

Emerging Readers
(no flags)

Beginning Readers
(1 flag)

Transitional Readers
(2 flags)

Fluent Readers
(3 flags)

These levels are meant only as a guide. All levels are subject to change.

ABDO
Publishing Company

To see a complete list of SandCastle™ books and other nonfiction titles from ABDO Publishing Company, visit **www.abdopub.com** or contact us at:
4940 Viking Drive, Edina, Minnesota 55435 • 1-800-800-1312 • fax: 1-952-831-1632